M000266004

The Swan Song

By Kaye Graham

Illustrations by
Shelly Hehenberger

With an afterword by
Nikki Giovanni

Owl Canyon Press
Niwot, Colorado

The Swan Song ©2023 by Kaye Graham
Avec Vous ©2023 by Nikki Giovanni

First Edition, 2023
All Rights Reserved
Library of Congress Cataloging-in-Publication Data
Graham, Kaye
The Swan song —1st ed.
p. cm.
Format: (paperback)
ISBN: 978-1-952085-24-6
Retail Price: $18.95
Format: (Hardcover)
ISBN: 978-1-952085-25-3
Retail Price: $24.95
Library of Congress Control Number: 2023916009

For more information contact:
Gene Hayworth
Owl Canyon Press
(720) 412-1548
gene.hayworth@owlcanyonpress.com

Ordering information: Available from Ingram Book
Company, Baker & Taylor, Follett Library Resources,
and Brodart Company

Disclaimer
No part of this book may be reproduced in any form or by
any electronic or mechanical means including information
storage retrieval systems without permission in writing from
the publisher, except by a reviewer, who may quote brief
passages for review. Neither the authors, the publishers, nor
its dealers or distributors shall be liable to the purchaser
or any other person or entity with respect to any liability,
loss, or damage caused or alleged to be caused directly or
indirectly by this book.

The Swan Song

By Kaye Graham

Illustrations by
Shelly Hehenberger

With an afterword by
Nikki Giovanni

Owl Canyon Press
Niwot, Colorado

For Peter

Each day, every day, always

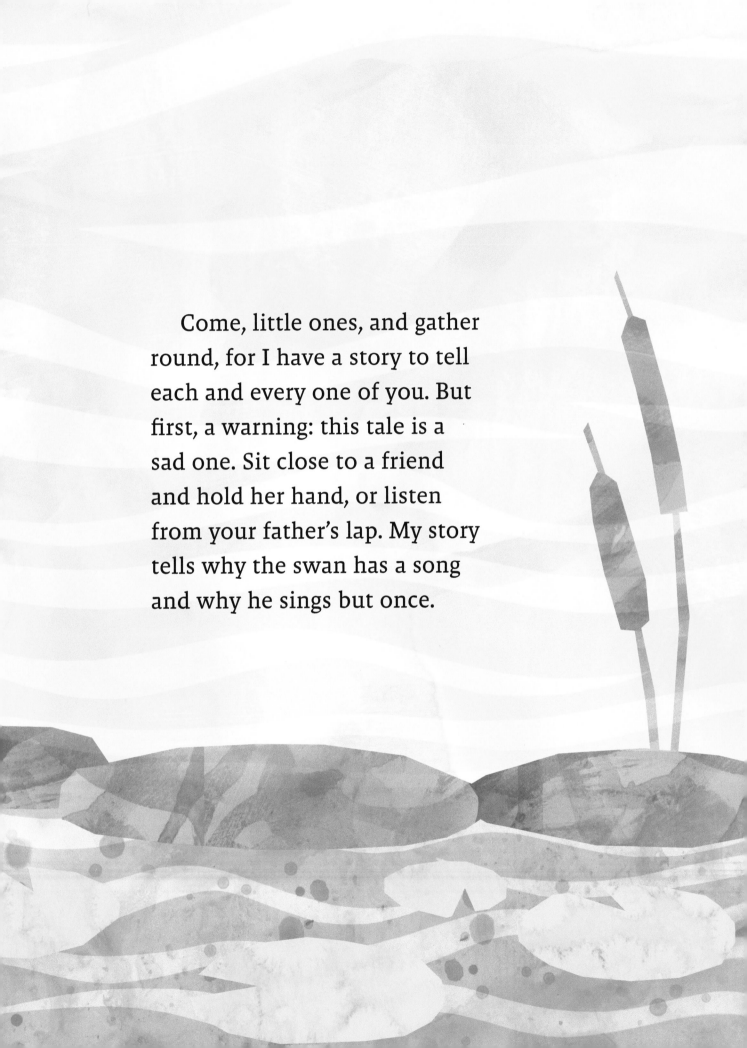

Come, little ones, and gather round, for I have a story to tell each and every one of you. But first, a warning: this tale is a sad one. Sit close to a friend and hold her hand, or listen from your father's lap. My story tells why the swan has a song and why he sings but once.

Long, long ago the first day dawned on a new world. What a beautiful world it came to be—sunrise, noon and sunset, starry skies and moon at night, blue ocean depths, tiny violet and mighty oak, fish of the sea, animals of the land, and birds of the air.

Birds were not yet the birds you recognize today. Every bird had his or her wings and feathers, each had a beak or a bill, and they all looked much the same. One morning at the dawn of time, the giver of wishes and dreams gathered the birds and, clad in her rainbow robe, stood ready to hear what each feathered creature might want.

The cardinal was a bold bird who knew exactly what he desired. "Color me red, if it please you Madam. I long to flash like fire as I dart through the forest."

"No fair," cried the tanager, "I too wish to be red."

The wishgiver smiled and granted their wishes. She also gave the cardinal a saucy crest to set him apart from the tanager.

"Perhaps a wee splash of red for me," begged the robin and the blackbird. The giver of wishes and dreams allowed one a red breast and the other scarlet epaulettes at the wing.

The birds were delighted to see these fine changes and clustered closer to the wishgiver.

"Blue, blue," cried the jay and the bunting, and their wishes were instantly granted.

"Pink for me, please." Uttering these words, the tall flamingo blushed, arched her neck, and admired herself from every angle.

All colors exhausted, the birds dreamed on. The nightingale asked for a melodious voice. The eagle sought to soar the highest. Ducks wanted webbed feet so that they could swim as well as fly. The more the birds dreamed and wished, the more beauty and variety appeared upon the earth.

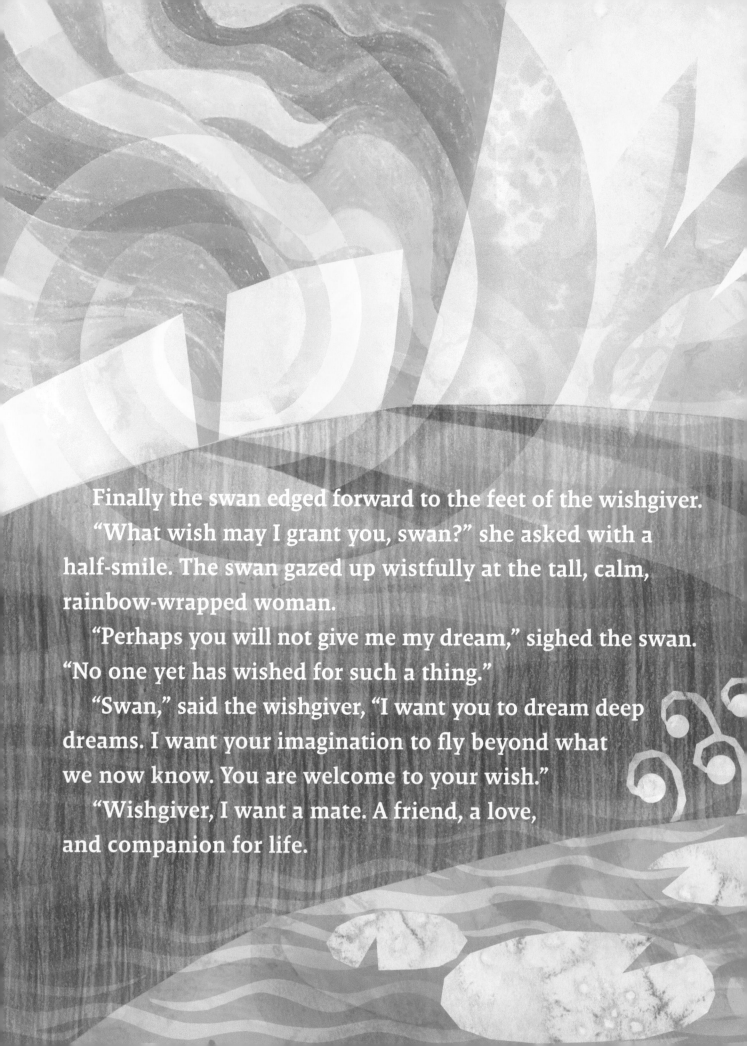

Finally the swan edged forward to the feet of the wishgiver.

"What wish may I grant you, swan?" she asked with a half-smile. The swan gazed up wistfully at the tall, calm, rainbow-wrapped woman.

"Perhaps you will not give me my dream," sighed the swan. "No one yet has wished for such a thing."

"Swan," said the wishgiver, "I want you to dream deep dreams. I want your imagination to fly beyond what we now know. You are welcome to your wish."

"Wishgiver, I want a mate. A friend, a love, and companion for life.

The giver of wishes and dreams gazed down
sadly. In all her wisdom, she had not expected
the swan, or indeed any bird, to ask for one
deep, abiding love. She drew the folds of her
rainbow robe closely around her and paced
alone at the forest's edge. The birds watched
anxiously. Would the swan get his wish?
Why was the wishgiver reluctant to answer?

Finally she walked back to the gathered birds. "Swan," she said, "you have made a beautiful wish. I do not think that you understand all that you have wished for, but I will grant you your heart's desire. And I will give you an unasked gift as well: to sing one song, that you will sing but once. When you sing, the world will stop to listen."

Beside himself with joy, the swan began to seek his one true mate. Soon enough his dream came true as he found the swan to cherish as his lifelong companion.

The swans made their home on a willow-fringed island in a reed-fringed lake. Father Cob and Mother Pen were devoted to one another and to their cygnets, what the world calls baby swans. Every day the swan family would paddle around the lake with the cygnets bobbing behind until one might grow tired and finish the outing on a parent's back.

The cygnets would grow large, find their own mates, and fly away to other islands and other lakes. Cob and Pen watched their grown brood go with some sadness, but after all they had each other. With every passing day their love grew deeper and stronger.

Season followed season. Spring would find
Pen sitting on five or six eggs in her nest.
In summer the swans would dart and glide
on the lake's smooth surface.

In fall they watched the geese fly south
overhead, and in winter they kept one
another snug and warm in their home on
the island. So the seasons passed into years.

One autumn morning Pen showed no interest in the migration of the geese. Instead she shivered and sighed. Finally, calling her companion to her side, she said, "My friend and my love, I feel so strange. I do not know the word for what is happening, but I fear that my years, seasons, and days are coming to an end."

Cob looked upon her with terror and dismay. "Surely I can do something to help you," he cried. He called the oldest of the cygnet brood to him and dispatched him at once to find the giver of wishes and dreams. "Bring her here at once. Tell her I must have one more wish. I cannot lose my mate."

The young swan flew off as fast as his wings would take him, and he searched the forest for the wishgiver. Finally he caught a glimpse of her rainbow robe and, with a mighty beating of wings, descended to the spot where she stood.

"Please come," he gasped. "My mother is ill, and my father is beside himself with grief. He must see you to make one last wish."

The wishgiver looked sadly at the young swan. "I know why you have come," said she. "I cannot help your mother now. She is about to die. When your father asked for a mate for life, he did not know as I know that one day life ceases to be. His beautiful dream led to deepest happiness, and now it will become his deepest sorrow. When you return to your father, remind him of my gift. Don't forget," she called as the young swan departed for the air. "Remember the gift."

When the young swan returned to the island in the lake, he found his father sitting beside the still, cold body of his mate. Dazed and mute, his heart like a heavy stone, Cob felt that he could sink beneath the surface of the lake and never float or fly again.

"Why didn't the wishgiver come?" he asked in despair. "She gave me my mate, but she did not tell me that I could not keep her forever. Where is she? She must give me back my mate again."

"She says she cannot," his son sadly replied. "But she told me to remind you of her gift."

"Her gift? I do not remember a gift. I never wanted anything but my companion and dearest love. I asked for no gift but my mate." Then, slowly, Cob started to remember. "A song. The wishgiver said that I would sing one beautiful song. Ah, I remember now. She said that I would sing just one time and that the world would stop and listen."

Even remembering the gift, the swan felt uncertain. Oh, he had honked and called, but he had never tried to sing. Why should he sing? And if he did, how should he begin? What would he sing about? The sadness of his loss settled full upon him. He wished that he too were cold and quiet, unable to feel the overflowing pain in his heart.

Finally he tried one long, low note
that floated out over the lake. The shore
birds stopped at the strange new sound.

The swan tried again. Higher this
time and longer was his note, and the
forest animals pricked up their ears.

The swan began to sing the story of his life. In lovely, lilting melody he sang of his wish for a mate. His voice soared triumphantly as he sang of their years of love and companionship. Humans on the shore heard and reached for one another's hands.

The swan sang of the hatching of cygnets,
the pleasure of swimming and flight, the beauty
of his island home, the changing of the seasons.
The world listened in trembling awe to a song
that none had heard before.

Finally, the swan sang of his gratitude
to the wishgiver, for he knew that it was
better to love and suffer than to live without
connection to another heart and soul.

As his last notes lingered on the frosty
air, the swan bowed his head and tucked it
under his wing. His one swan song was over.
His mighty and loving heart ceased beating.
Both swans were still.

The young cob looked sadly upon his parents, but he had a mate of his own and it was time to fly home to her. He now knew that life and love do not go on forever. But when the moment of sad parting came, his heart was prepared to sing.

So now, little ones, you know
why we speak of the swan's song
and why he sings but once.

Avec Vous

(Afterword for Kaye)

My Latin is limited
My Greek is worse
And the languages
And signs
The drawings
The bones
We find

Some neatly buried
Some spread Apart
Perhaps by storm
Perhaps War
Maybe big animals
Looking for a meal
Maybe the ants
Or underground life
   forever
Looking for a home

Maybe just two lovers
Holding on
To each other
As the fire burns
Or rocks roll over
As planes fall
Or even water with all
Its force
Pushing mud
Or tree roots
Or something
But not the Love
That holds the two
Together

And they whisper
To each other

Don't wait for me
I'll be there

....

Nikki Giovanni

KAYE GRAHAM

A teacher and scholar focusing on children's literature, Kathryn V. (Kaye) Graham has devised and offered courses on Ethnic Literature for Children, Children's Literature and Film, the Harry Potter Phenomenon, and Award-winning Children's Books in Virginia Tech's English Department and Lifelong Learning Institute. *The Swan Song* is her first children's book. The draft of the story came into being when Kaye was auditing friend and colleague Nikki Giovanni's seminar on writing for a young audience.

NIKKI GIOVANNI is an American poet, activist, and author who has written many books for young people, including *I Am Loved*, *Rosa*, a Caldecott Honor Book, and most recently *A Library*. The first recipient of the Rosa L. Parks Woman of Courage Award, Nikki also won the Langston Hughes Medal for Poetry. She is University Distinguished Professor Emerita at Virginia Tech. "Avec Vous" is Nikki's lyric response to Kaye's story.

SHELLY HEHENBERGER

The illustrations in this book were created using hand-painted textures and patterns (acrylic on paper) that have been collaged digitally in Adobe Photoshop.

Shelly Hehenberger has been illustrating and writing children's books since 1996.

She has a BA in Graphic Design from Indiana University, 1990, and a Master of Fine Arts degree in Painting from the University of Cincinnati, 1994.

She is also an art teacher and abstract painter, to see her painting work please visit: www.shellyhehenberger.com

To see more of her illustration work please visit: www.shellyhehenbergerillustration.com

Printed in the USA
CPSIA information can be obtained
at www.ICGtesting.com
LVHW072354261023
761974LV00019B/288